Angular Observables and Promises

A Practical Guide to Asynchronous Programming

Abdelfattah Ragab

Angular Observables and Promises

A Practical Guide to Asynchronous Programming

Abdelfattah Ragab

Introduction

Welcome to the book "Angular Observables and Promises: A Practical Guide to Asynchronous Programming".
In this book, I explain how to use observables and promises effectively for asynchronous programming.
I show you practical scenarios and explain when you should use them and which operators you need to use.
I will give you best practices with important pointers that, when used correctly, can make all the difference and have a big impact on performance.
There are also things you should be aware of and avoid when working with observables, otherwise performance can be affected.
By the end of this book, you will be able to use Observables and Promises in your Angular application and handle all kinds of scenarios.
Let us get started.

What are Signals?

Signals are a new feature in Angular that improves the reactivity of the framework and the detection of changes.
Signals are used for **synchronous** operations, so you should use them to manage state and update the user interface efficiently.

I mentioned them at the beginning to illustrate the role they play in Angular. I will not go into them in this book, as synchronous operations are not the topic of this book. I will mainly focus on the asynchronous operations.

What is RxJS?

RxJS (Reactive Extensions for JavaScript) is a powerful reactive programming library that uses observables to manage asynchronous data streams. It enables developers to work with asynchronous operations in a declarative style, making it easier to handle complex data streams and events.

What are Observables?

Observables are part of the RxJS library that allow you to handle asynchronous **data streams**.

What are Promises?

A promise in JavaScript is an object that represents the eventual completion or failure of an asynchronous operation.
A promise handles **one single value**.

new Promise

Most of the time, Promises and Observables are created for you by libraries, http, Apis and so on. But if you want to create one yourself, you can use the constructor. Let's look at how to create a promise with the constructor. It takes a function with two parameters: **resolve** and **reject**. Call resolve if the asynchronous operation succeeds, and reject if it fails.

```javascript
myPromise = new Promise((resolve,
reject) => {
  setTimeout(() => {
    const success = true;
    if (success) {
      resolve('Resolved');
    } else {
      reject('Rejected');
    }
  }, 3000);
});
```

```
Promise.resolve()
```

You can create a successful promise using

```
Promise.resolve().
const promise=
Promise.resolve('Resolved');
```

```
Promise.reject()
```

Similarly, you can create a rejected promise using

```
Promise.reject().
const promise =
Promise.reject('Rejected');
```

Using Promises

Use `.then()` **to handle the resolved state and** `.catch()` **to handle the rejected state.**

```
this.promise
  .then((result: any) => {
    console.log(result);
  })
  .catch((error: any) => {
    console.error(error);
  });
```

Async/Await

Async/Await offers a more readable way of working with asynchronous code than is possible with `.then()` and `.catch()`.
It consists of two parts in order to function:
- Declare the outer function as async. Simply add the word `async` in front of the function name.
- Use the word `await` when you call the promise.

```
async fetchData() {
  const result = await
this.productService.getProduct(1);
  console.log(result);
  return result;
}
```

new Observable

You can create an observable using the constructor:

```
myObservable = new
Observable((subscriber) => {
  subscriber.next('First value');
  subscriber.next('Second value');

  subscriber.complete();
});
```

Unlike Promises, which are created within JavaScript and do not require imports, you need to import Observables from `'rxjs'`.

`of`

To create an observable that outputs the specified values.
```
myObservable = of(1, 2, 3);
```

`from`

To convert various data types into observables.
```
myObservable = from(myPromise)
```

`HTTP` returns observables

All `HttpClient` methods return observables.
```
myObservable =
this.http.get('https://api.examp..');
```

Subscribe to an Observable

To subscribe to an observable, use the `subscribe` method, which takes up to three arguments:

- **next**: called whenever the observable outputs a new value.
- **error**: called in case of errors.

- **`complete`**: called when the observable is
  completed.

```
this.myObservable.subscribe({
  next: (value: any) => {
    console.log(value);
  },
  complete: () => {
    console.log('Observable
completed.');
  },
  error: (e: any) => {
    console.log(e);
  },
});
```

unsubscribe

When you subscribe to an observable, it returns a
subscription object. This object can be used to
unsubscribe from the observable, which is important to
avoid memory leaks, especially in Angular components.

```
this.subscription =
this.myObservable.subscribe(..);
```

Unsubscribe when the component is destroyed.

```
ngOnDestroy(): void {
  if (this.subscription)
this.subscription.unsubscribe();
}
```

Cold Observables

Cold observables are a type of observable in RxJS that **only output values when a subscriber subscribes to them**. This means that data production is directly linked to the subscription process. Each subscriber to a cold observable receives their own independent execution of the observable, which can lead to different results depending on when they subscribe to it.
Common examples of cold observables are HTTP requests.

Hot Observables

Hot observables are a type of observable in RxJS that **generate values regardless of whether there are subscribers**. This means that data is generated independently of the subscription process.

All subscribers share the same version of the observable. This means that if several subscribers establish a connection to a hot observable, they all receive the same output values from this point onwards, but no values that were output before they logged in.

Common examples of hot observables are events such as mouse movements or keystrokes.

```
hotObservable = new Subject();
```

BehaviorSubject

Similar to Subject, BehaviorSubject is also a **hot** observable.
It starts emitting values as soon as it is created, regardless of whether there are subscribers.
All subscribers to a BehaviorSubject share the same instance, i.e. they receive the same output values from the moment they subscribe.

```
behaviorSubject = new
BehaviorSubject('Initial Value');
```

Subject vs BehaviorSubject

	Subject	BehaviorSubject
Initial value	no	yes
Current value	no	yes

Initial value

- **Subject:** A subject has no initial value. When a subscriber subscribes to a subject, they only receive the values that are sent after their subscription. If no values have been sent yet, they will not receive any.

- **BehaviorSubject:** A BehaviorSubject requires an initial value when it is created. This means that each subscriber receives the initial value immediately after the subscription as well as all subsequent values that are issued after the subscription.

Current value

- **Subject:** A subject does not remember the last value sent. If a subscriber completes a subscription after some values have already been sent, they miss these previous values and only receive the new values that were sent after their subscription.
- **BehaviorSubject:** A BehaviorSubject retains the last value sent. When a new subscriber subscribes, they immediately receive the latest value so that they are always informed of the current status.

Async pipe (| `async`)

The async pipe provides a simple way to process asynchronous data streams directly in the template.

Advantages of the async pipe

The async pipe **automatically subscribes** to the observable when the template is rendered **and unsubscribes** when the component is destroyed. This helps to avoid memory leaks and simplifies your code as you do not have to manage the subscriptions manually.

By using the asynchronous pipe, you can **bind directly** to observable data **in your templates** without the need for additional logic in your component code. This results in cleaner and more readable templates.

```
@if (data$ | async; as data) {
  <p>{{ data.title }}</p>
}
```

The async pipe supports Angular's change detection mechanism. When the observable outputs a new value, the async pipe triggers change detection and updates the view automatically. This **minimizes the need for manual change detection** strategies.

RxJS operators

RxJS operators are pure functions that allow you to manipulate and transform data streams represented by observables.
Operators can be combined with each other to create complex data processing pipelines. This combinability is

one of the strengths of RxJS, allowing you to create sophisticated asynchronous workflows with ease.

Hands on

Enough theory, now let's write some code and see how you would need RxJS in practice.

Distributed data

A common scenario is that you need to make many API calls to get all the data on the page. Let's say you are working on an online e-commerce business and for some reason you have decided to split the product data into multiple units. You store the main product details in the product entity, which contains the productId, name, price, etc.
In another entity, you store the product media with details of images, videos, resources, etc.
And in a third entity you store variations of the product, such as sizes, colors, models and so on.
Each entity can be accessed via its own API endpoint. To be able to display the product on the page, you must first receive a response from all these endpoints before you can display the product.

forkJoin

`forkJoin` allows you to combine multiple observables and wait for them all to complete before outputting their last values as an array.

Once all observables are completed, `forkJoin` outputs an array containing the last values output by each observable. If an observable does not send a value before completion, `forkJoin` does not include the value of that observable in the array sent.

If one of the inner observables fails, `forkJoin` will abort immediately and you will lose the values of any other observables that may have completed successfully. It is therefore important to handle errors in the observables that are passed to `forkJoin` accordingly.

```
fetchData() {
  const req1 =
this.http.get('https://api../product/1')
;
  const req2 =
this.http.get('https://api../media/1');
  const req3 =
this.http.get('https://api../variations/
1');
```

```typescript
    forkJoin([req1, req2,
req3]).subscribe(
    (results: any) => {
      const product = results[0];
      const media = results[1];
      const variations = results[2];
      console.log(product, media,
variations);
    },
    (error) => {
      console.error(error);
    }
  );
}
```

In this example, `forkJoin` waits for all three `HTTP` requests to complete and then outputs an array with the responses. If one of the requests fails, error handling is triggered in the subscription.

combineLatest

The `combineLatest` operator combines the latest values of several observables. It outputs an array of the latest values as soon as one of the observables entered outputs a new value. This operator is useful if you want to react to changes in several observables.

merge

The `merge` operator combines several observables into a single observable that outputs all the values of the input observables as soon as they arrive. In contrast to `forkJoin`, it does not wait until all observables are completed.

Mapping data

When working with some applications, you may find that the backend already sends you all the data you need, but for some reason you want it in a slightly different organization. You can easily achieve this with the `map` operator.

map

The `map` operator transforms each value emitted by an observable by applying a specified function.
Let's say you are receiving the product object like this from the backend

```
{
  id: 1,
  name: 'Product 1',
  color: [
    {
      value: '#2546fa',
    },
```

```
    {
      value: '#5786fa',
    },
  ],
}
```

But you want it like this:

```
{
  id: 1,
  name: 'Product 1',
  colors: ['#2546fa', '#5786fa'],
}
```

Here it is:

```
this.http
.get('https://api.examp../product/1')
  .pipe(
    map((product: any) => {
      return {
        id: product.id,
        name: product.name,
        colors: product.color.map((c:
any) => c.value),
      };
    })
  )
  .subscribe((product) =>
console.log(product));
```

FYI: JavaScript has a similar method with the same name `map` that works for arrays. You can convert array elements using the map function, like I did with the color array to convert it from an array of objects to an array of strings.

filter

You can use the `filter` operator to output only those values that fulfill a certain condition.

```
this.http
  .get('https://api.examp../products')
    .pipe(filter((product: any) =>
product.price > 1000))
    .subscribe((product) =>
console.log(product));
```

take

You can use the `take` operator to take the first n values output by an observable and then complete them.

```
this.http
.get('https://api.example.com/product/im
ages/1')
    .pipe(take(3))
    .subscribe((product) =>
console.log(product));
```

first

The `first` operator outputs the first value emitted by the observable source.

```
this.http
.get('https://api.example.com/product/1'
)
  .pipe(first())
  .subscribe((product) =>
console.log(product));
```

first() vs take(1)

The `first()` operator triggers an error if the
observable is completed without a value being output.
`take(1)` does not raise an error if the observable is
completed without outputting a value; it is simply
completed without outputting anything.

tap

The `tap` operator has no influence on the results. It only
allows you to access the response if you want to log or
debug the values without changing the output values.

```
this.http
.get('https://api.examp../product/1')
  .pipe(tap((product: any) =>
console.log('Product: ', product)))
  .subscribe((product) =>
console.log(product));
```

debounceTime

The `debounceTime` operator is useful for limiting the rate at which values are output. It outputs a value from the observable source only after a certain period of silence.

This is very useful in text input scenarios where you should wait until the user has completed the search query before performing the search.

ReactiveForms uses RxJS for `valueChanges` events. You simply subscribe to the `valueChanges` event and with the debounceTime operator you can limit the call rate of the backend service. You can be sure that it will only be called once at the end of the specified debounceTime.

```
this.form
  .get('search')
  ?.valueChanges.pipe(debounceTime(800))
  .subscribe((query: any) => {
    console.log(query);
  });
```

switchMap

The `switchMap` operator is used to switch to a new observable as soon as the source observable outputs a new value. It cancels all running inner observables and ensures that only the last value sent is processed. This is particularly useful in scenarios such as search inputs where you want to discard previous requests when a new one is received.

```
this.http
  .post('https://api.examp../search', {
query })
  .pipe(switchMap((product: any) =>
of(product)))
  .subscribe((product) =>
console.log(product));
```

exhaustMap

The operator `exhaustMap` ignores new emissions from the source observable as long as an inner observable is still active. Once the inner observable is completed, it will process the next emission from the source. This is useful in scenarios where you want to prevent overlapping requests, e.g. when a user quickly clicks a button several times.

concatMap

The `concatMap` operator places the inner observables in a queue and processes them one after the other in the order in which they were received. It waits until the current inner observable is completed before continuing with the next one. This is useful if the order of emissions is important and you want to ensure that each observable is completed before starting the next one.

mergeMap

The `mergeMap` operator makes it possible for several inner observables to be active at the same time and to output the values after their arrival. This is useful if you want to process multiple simultaneous requests without waiting for each one to complete.

catchError

This operator is used to intercept and handle errors in the stream of observation data. It enables a new observable to be returned or an error to be thrown. This is comparable to a try-catch block in synchronous code.

```
this.http

.get('https://api.example.com/product/1'
)
  .pipe(
    catchError((error) => {
      console.error('Error occurred:',
error);
      return of(undefined);
    })
  )
  .subscribe((data) =>
console.log(data));
```

Important considerations

Use `first()`

If you create an observable in the click event, remember to log out before exiting the handler method. You can easily do this with the `first()` or `take(1)` operators. If you forget to do this, more subscriptions will be loaded into memory with each click, which will affect performance.

```
onClick() {
  this.productsService
    .getAll()
    .pipe(first())
    .subscribe((products: any) =>
(this.products = products));
}
```

After getting the first value the subscription will be completed. This means that you do not need to manually unsubscribe from the observable, as the subscription will be terminated after the first emission.

Unsubscribe in the `ngOnDestroy`

Always ensure that you unsubscribe from observables in the `ngOnDestroy` lifecycle hook.

Avoid nested subscriptions

Nested subscriptions can lead to complex code that is difficult to maintain. Instead of subscribing within another subscription, use higher order mapping operators such as `switchMap`, `mergeMap` or `concatMap` to smooth out the observable streams.

Handle errors gracefully

Always handle errors in your observable streams. Use the `catchError` operator to handle errors properly and avoid unhandled exceptions that can crash your application.

async pipe

Use `async` pipes in component templates. This promotes clean code, efficient subscription management and automatic change detection.

Conclusion

Congratulations! You have read the book "Angular Observables and Promises: A Practical Guide to Asynchronous Programming". Now you are able to handle all asynchronous scenarios with ease.

Remember that learning Angular is an ongoing process. Practice makes perfect — create your own projects, experiment with the features you have learned, and delve into the extensive online resources.

Thank you for joining me in my exploration of Angular. I wish you the best of luck on your programming journey. Have fun programming and good luck with your applications!

Media Attributions

Gradient asynchronous work illustration
Image by pikisuperstar on Freepik

Modern annual report magazine page flyer a company
catalog
Image by starline on Freepik

Don't miss out!

Receive an email when Abdelfattah Ragab publishes a new book. It's free and without obligation.

Also by Abdelfattah Ragab

Shippo is a multi-carrier shipping solution designed to streamline the shipping process for businesses of all sizes.

By integrating shipping into your application, you can create better types of e-commerce applications.

You will learn how to create the labels, calculate shipping costs, and get the fastest, cheapest, and best rates.

By the end of the book, you will be able to enable shipping in your Angular application and handle all kinds of scenarios.

Stripe Integration in Angular

Stripe is a leading payment processing platform that enables businesses to accept online payments.
By integrating payment processing into your application, you can create all kinds of e-commerce applications.

You will learn how to create the checkout session, how to use webhooks events and finally how to go live. By the end of the book, you will be able to process payments in your Angular application and handle all kinds of scenarios.

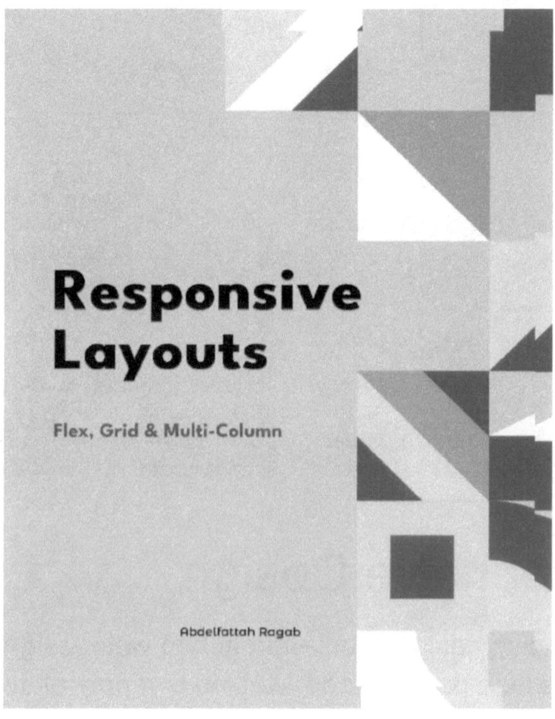

Responsive Design

Responsive design is an approach to web design that ensures web pages render well on a variety of devices and screen sizes, from desktop monitors to mobile phones. The primary goal of responsive design is to provide an optimal viewing experience, making it easy for users to read and navigate the site with minimal resizing, panning, and scrolling.

To learn more about responsive design, I advise you to read my book "**Responsive Layouts: Flex, Grid and Multi-Column**"
And read my book "**Responsive Design: All CSS responsive features**"

"**Angular Portfolio App Development**" will teach you how to create an online portfolio app that you can use to show off your skills to the world and your potential employers.

Angular Shopping Store

From Scratch to Successful Payment

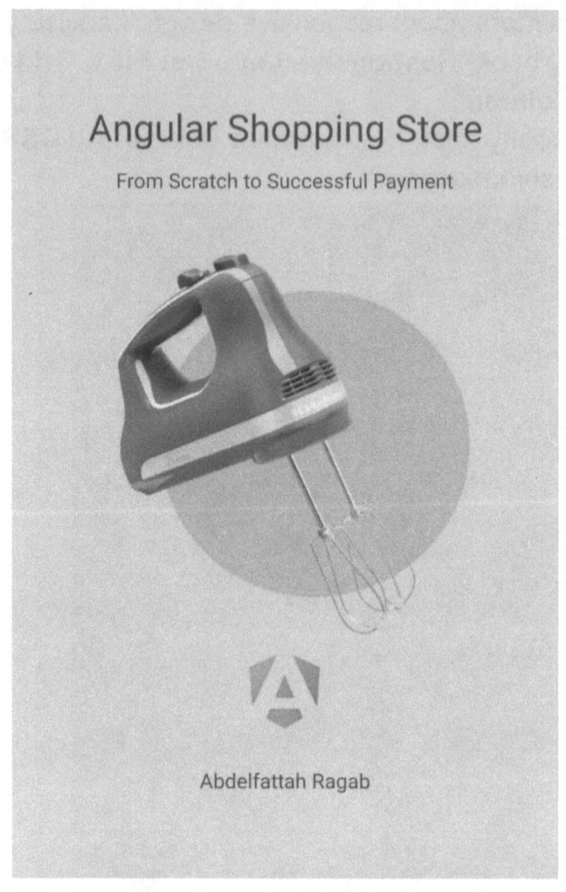

Abdelfattah Ragab

"**Angular Shopping Store**" a simple Angular e-commerce store.

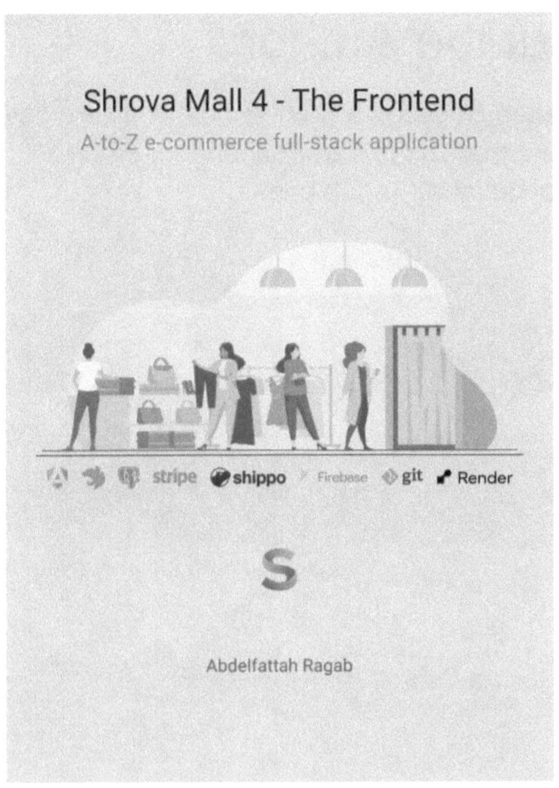

Once you are familiar with Angular, I recommend reading the book "**Shrova Mall**". This is a complete e-commerce solution that allows you to ship products to customers and accept payments online, among other things.

About the Author

Abdelfattah Ragab is a professional software developer with more than 20 years of experience. https://abdelfattah-ragab.com

About the Publisher

Abdelfattah Ragab is a highly qualified and experienced software developer with over 20 years of experience in the industry. Specializing in front-end development, Abdelfattah Ragab has a deep understanding of Angular, JavaScript, TypeScript, HTML and CSS.
Read more at https://abdelfattah-ragab.com